PRO

LEARN DRUMS WITH LESSON PLAN

BOOK 3/3

1. Edition 2023

ISBN 978-3-949357-16-9

Audio Tracks and Bonus Videos produced by RC Schneider

Design, layout and translation by RC Schneider

Rudiments notated by Kai-Ole Buuck

Photos by Thommy Buccini

Editing by Julia Stadler

Second lector Lisa Schneider

Coverfoto by Andrey Armyagov

Produced in Germany

Printed by AMAZON KDP

360 Drums | www.360drums.net | mail@360drums.net

LESSON PLAN WITH TOPIC OVERVIEW

The "Learn Drums with Lesson Plan" book series consists of three books: The **BASIC** book for beginners, the **ADVANCED** book for experienced players and the **PRO** book for aspiring professionals.

The topics and contents of the books are didactically tested and structured.

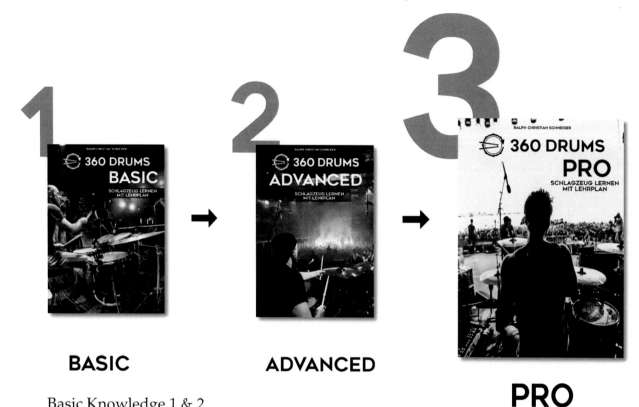

BASIC   ## ADVANCED   ## PRO

TOPICS

Basic Knowledge 1 & 2
Fill Ins 1, 2
Music Notation 1 & 2············> Music Notation 3············> **Music Notation 4**
Reading 1 & 2 ··················> Reading 3 ··················> **Reading 4**
Rock & Pop Grooves 1 & 2 ··> Rock & Pop Grooves 3
Hi-Hat 1 ························> Hi-Hat 2
Ghost Notes 1 & 2 ············> Ghost Notes 3
Chartreading 1 & 2············> Chartreading 3
Accents 1 ······················> Accents 2
                                Sixtuplets on the Set 1 & 2
                                Linear Drumming 1 & 2
                                Technique 1 & 2············> **Technique 3**
                                Rudiments 1 & 2············> **Rudiments 3**
                                Licks 1 & 2 ··················> **Licks 3 & 4**
                                Grooves & Styles 1··········> **Grooves & Styles 2 & 3**
                                Coordination 1 ··············> **Coordination 2**
                                                             Snare Solo 1 & 2
                                                             32nd on the Set 1 & 2
                                                             Improvisation 1 & 2
                                                             Polyrhythmics 1 & 2
                                                             Ostinatos 1 & 2
                                                             Drumsolo

Have you successfully mastered the **PRO** book?
Then get more books and content at www.360drums.net.

Audio Tracks & Bonus Videos

For most Grooves and exercises you will find an Audio Track to get an impression of how they sound.

You can download the tracks and videos from your account at

360 Drums or the direct link:

https://360drums.net/downloads

Notes for which there is an Audio Track are marked with this symbol.

Table of Contents

Table of Contents

Appendix

The 40 PAS Rudiments

Blank Sheet of Music

Practice Log

Online Videos

Preface

Dear drummers,

the **PRO** book is the crowning conclusion of the three-part series "Learn Drums with Lesson Plan". Those who have come this far and have practised through the **BASIC** and **ADVANCED** books can already be very proud of themselves. But now it's time not to rest on your successes, but to tackle and master the difficult challenges in the PRO book. In this book, mainly 32nd notes, Licks, polyrhythms, Latin Grooves and the supreme disciplines of drum and Snare Drum solos are practised.

Anyone who deals with these in-depth topics will certainly already have a few years of experience and may even be toying with the idea of becoming a professional musician. This can be a very fulfilling profession. If the basic requirements are right, you are passionate about it and burn for it, I am firmly convinced that anyone is good enough and can be successful.

We are also fortunate these days to have many good schools and training institutions that can guide you along the way. The range of workshops and training courses is also growing steadily. In the past, until the beginning of the 90s, there was mainly training in classical percussion. The rock/pop/jazz direction had not yet arrived in the schools. We can be grateful for all the pioneers who brought these new structures into being back then.

I would like to encourage everyone to pursue their musical goals intensively and to dare to strive for a career in the music business. The music business is very diverse and in addition to the performing artist, there are also music teachers, instrumental teachers, sound engineers, authors, consultants, course leaders, specialist sellers, instrument makers, band coaches, music producers, bookers, event managers, music managers, A&R managers, and so on. In other words, there is enough room for everyone who is really serious and willing to bring out the best in themselves.

I can only confirm this myself: There hasn't been a day when I haven't been happy to get up and do my work. For me, anyone who manages to make a living in the music business is a success story - even if you are not constantly in the spotlight, but rather active behind the scenes.

In this sense, have fun and success with the **PRO** book!

RC Schneider

Author of the books **BASIC**, **ADVANCED** & **PRO** and founder of 360 Drums

Music Notation 4

Overview of all Note Values

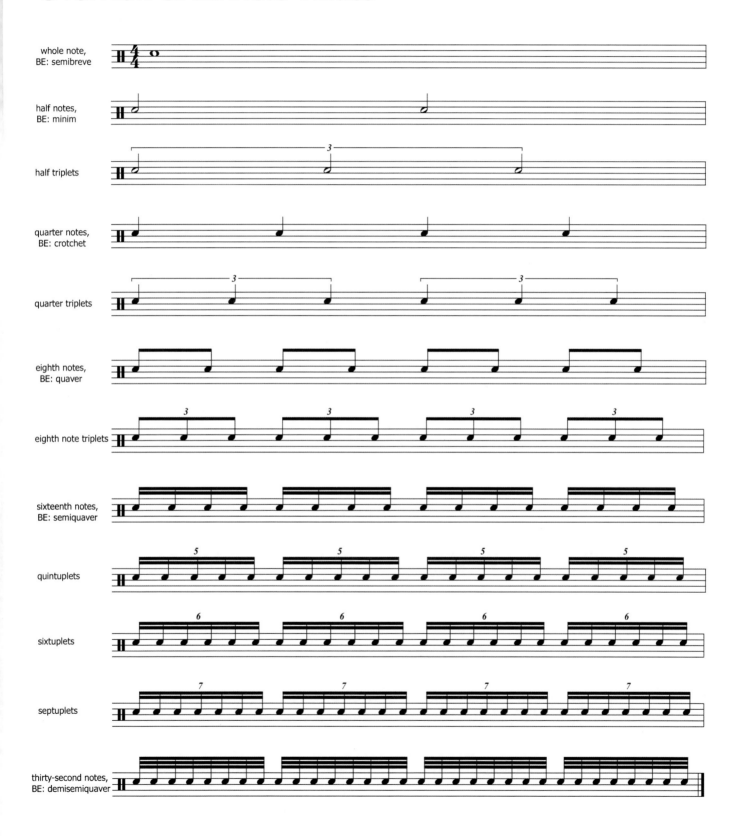

whole note, BE: semibreve

half notes, BE: minim

half triplets

quarter notes, BE: crotchet

quarter triplets

eighth notes, BE: quaver

eighth note triplets

sixteenth notes, BE: semiquaver

quintuplets

sixtuplets

septuplets

thirty-second notes, BE: demisemiquaver

Drum Notation & Key

There is no completely uniform system of notation. However, two principles have become established worldwide:

- The hi-hat is written at the top, the snare drum in the middle and the bass drum at the bottom (analogous to the basic structure of a drum kit).
- Cymbals are generally represented with a cross, drums with the note head filled in.

The basis of drum notes, which are immediately recognisable through the percussion clef, is the 5-line system familiar from "normal" notes.
Instead of different pitches, the individual instruments are notated on the lines and in the spaces. Each instrument is thus assigned a fixed position within the lines.

The rhythmic note values (quarter, eighth, sixteenth and two-thirtieth notes, triplets, quintuplets, septuplets etc., rests) correspond to the "normal" notes.

Drum Key:

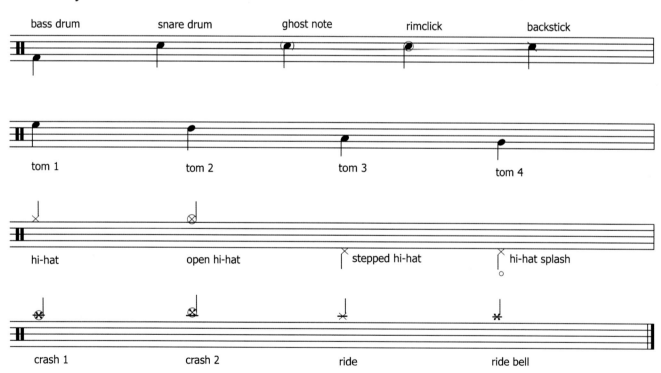

32nd Note Stickings

• Count quarter, eighth or 16th notes aloud

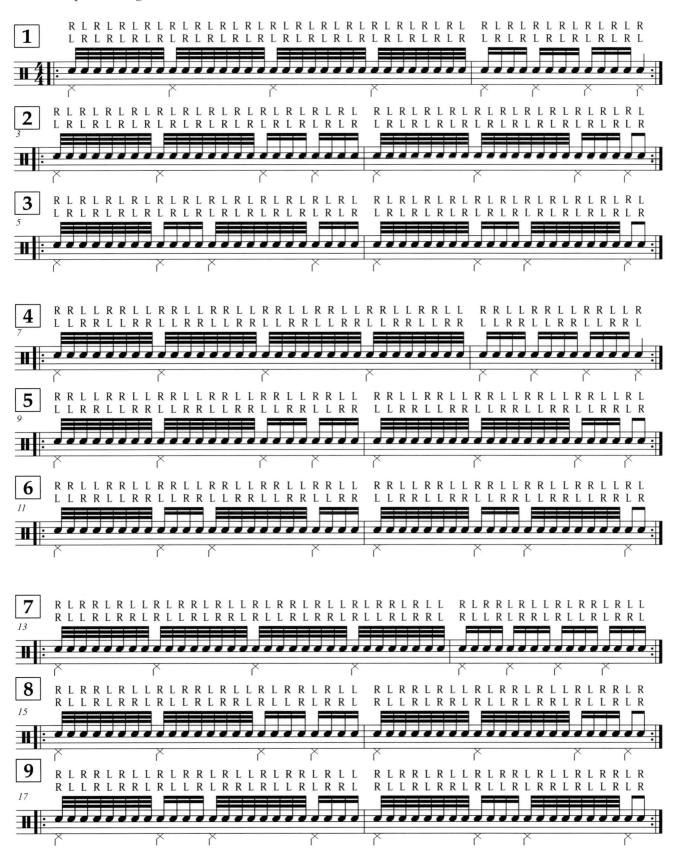

Reading 3

32nd

• Start slowly, the left foot taps the quarter note

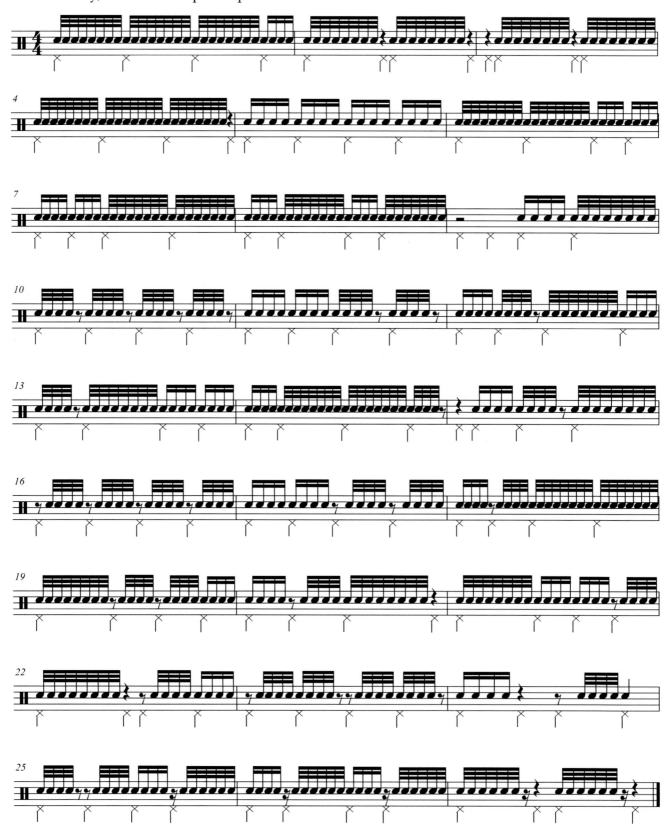

1 - 8 complete

- Count out loud or silently for yourself
- Count and clap the bars in advance
- The left foot runs along on the quarters

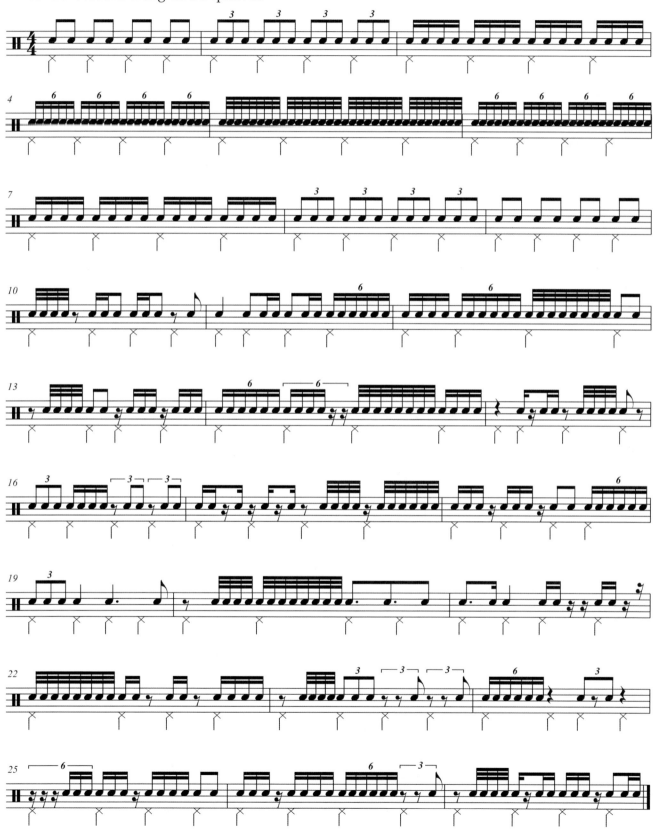

Rudiments 3

Hybrid Rudiments

Here is a selection of numerous hybrid rudiments that have become established over time. These rudiments are newer combinations of strokes and are not included in the 40 PAS Standard Rudiments.

1. Cheese (combination of Diddle and Flam)

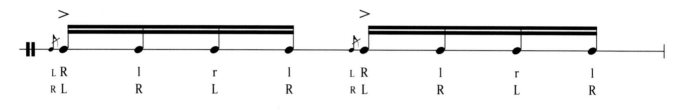

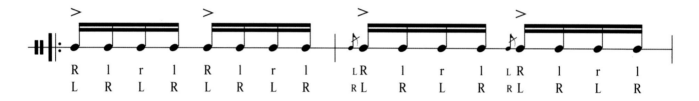

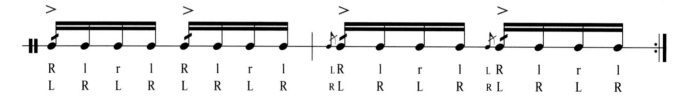

2. Cheese Paradiddle

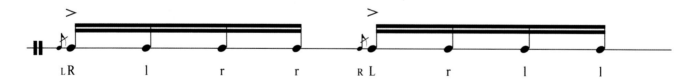

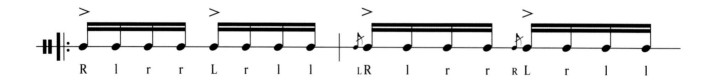

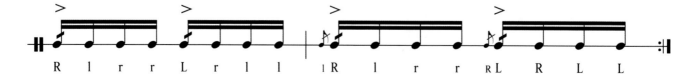

3. Flam Double Paradiddle

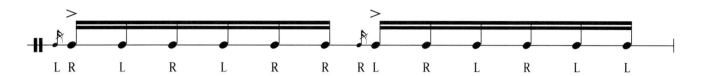

L R   L   R   L   R   R   R L   R   L   R   L   L

4. Cheese Double Paradiddle

L R   L   R   L   R   R   R L   R   L   R   L   L

L R   L   R   L   R   R   R L   R   L   R   L   L   L R   L   R   R

R L   R   L   R   L   L   L R   L   R   L   R   R   R L   R   L   L

5. Cheese Triple Paradiddle

L R   L   R   L   R   L   R   R   R L   R   L   R   L   R   L   L

L R   L   R   L   R   L   R   R   R L   R   L   R   L   R   L   L

L R   L   R   L   R   L   R   R   R L   R   L   R   L   R   L   L

Technique 3

AUDIO TRACK
#1

Paradiddle Progression

- The Paradiddle hand movement always remains the same
- Tap the quarter note with the left foot as well
- Start slowly and practise with metronome

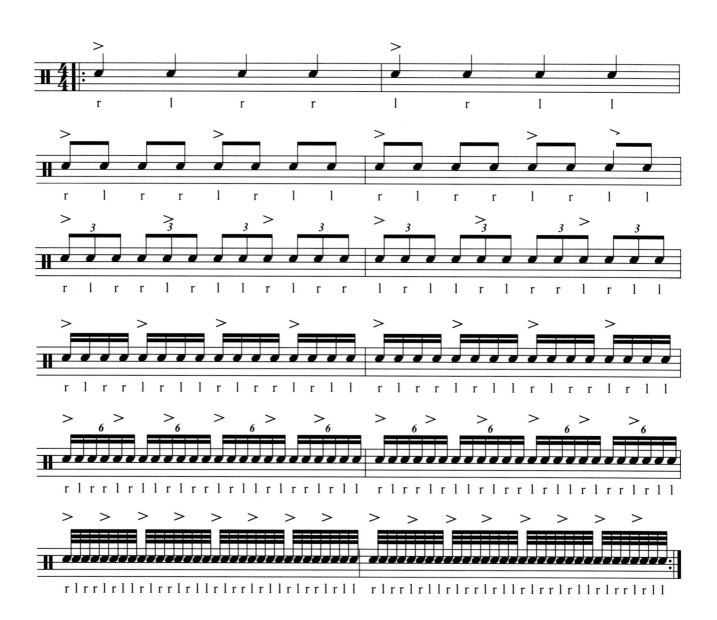

Six Stroke Roll Progression

- The Six Stroke Roll sticking always remains the same
- Tap the quarter note with the left foot as well
- Start slowly and practise with metronome

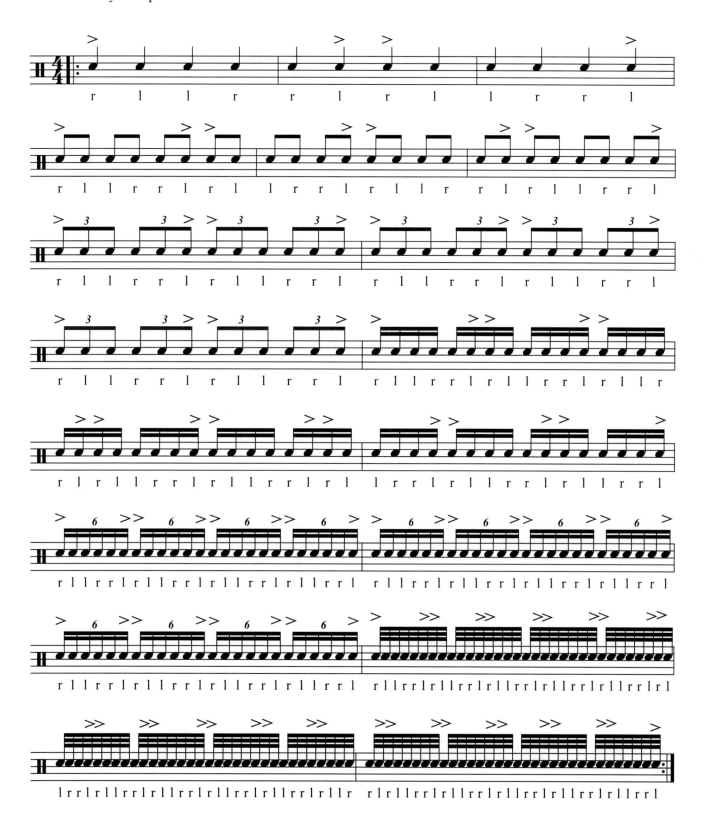

Backsticking

The backsticking technique is played by bringing the end of the stick forward through the opening of the hand and playing the strokes with it.

- The left foot taps on the quarter note with
- Practice long first and pay attention to a clean execution
- Practice with metronome

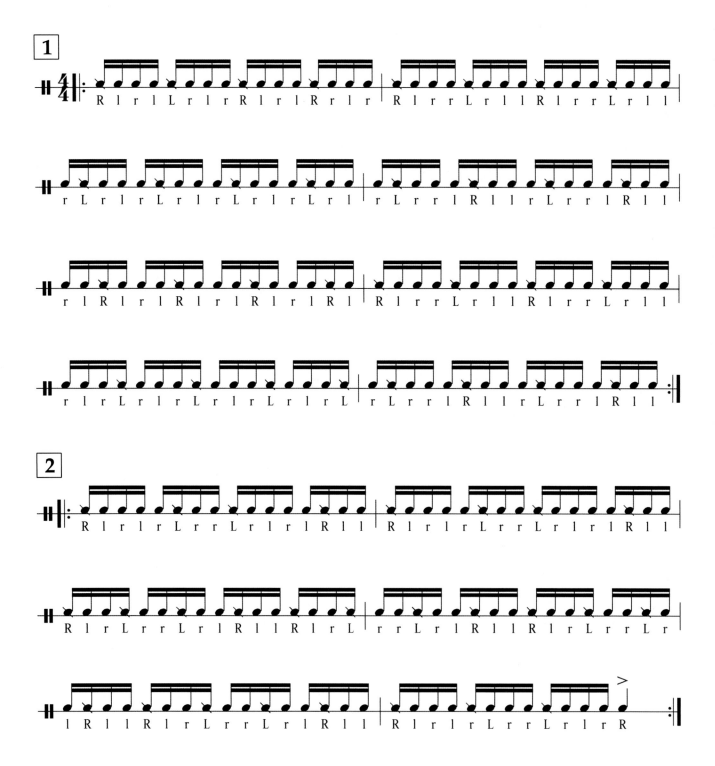

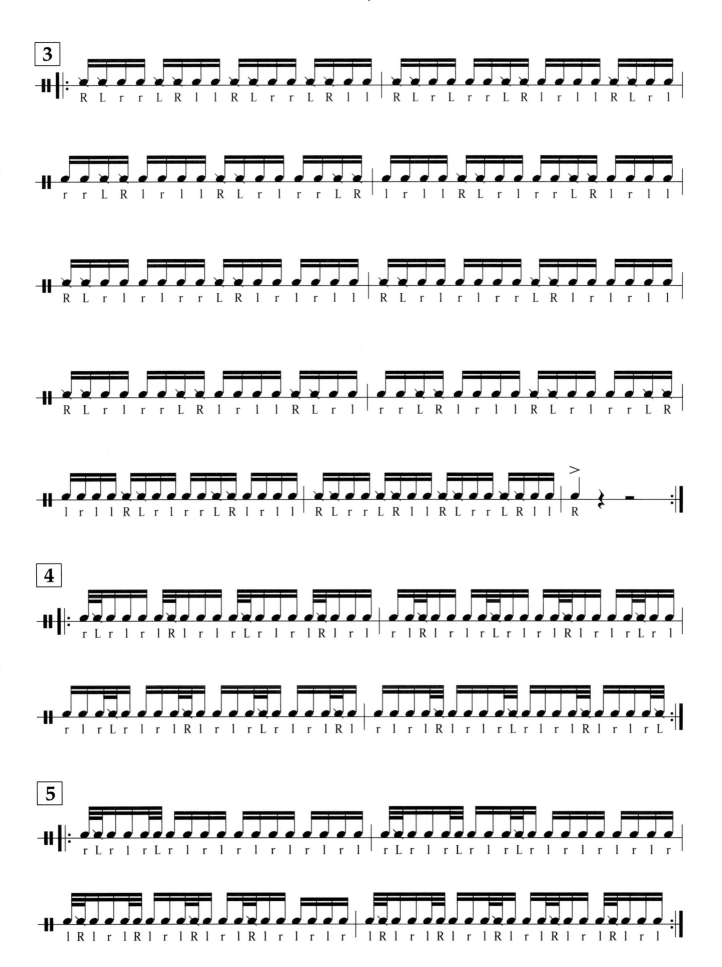

Snare Drum Solo 1

AUDIO TRACK #3

- Be careful not to neglect cleanliness and precision even at higher tempos
- Play each bar individually in a loop, then whole lines and finally the solo in one piece
- The left foot taps along with the quarter pulse

32nd on the Set 1

- Start slowly and practise with metronome
- Cut the pattern into quarter notes and practise each quarter note on its own
- The left foot taps along with the quarter pulse
- Play the patterns as a Fill In alternating with Grooves

Linear Pattern 1:

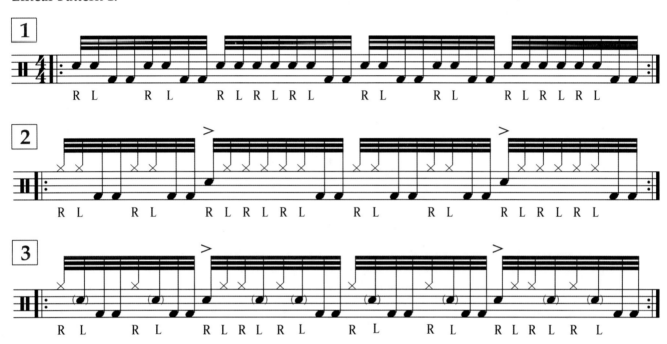

Linear Pattern 2:

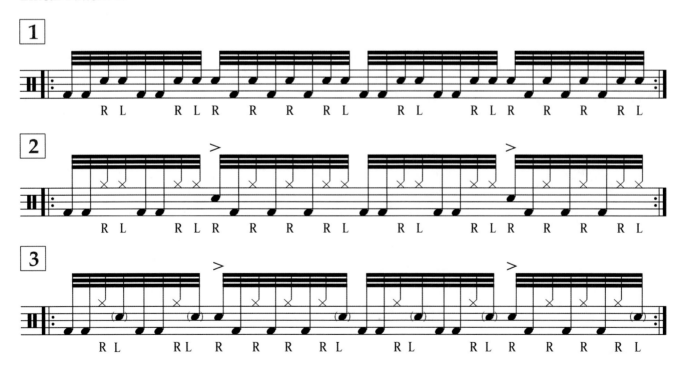

Linear Pattern 3:

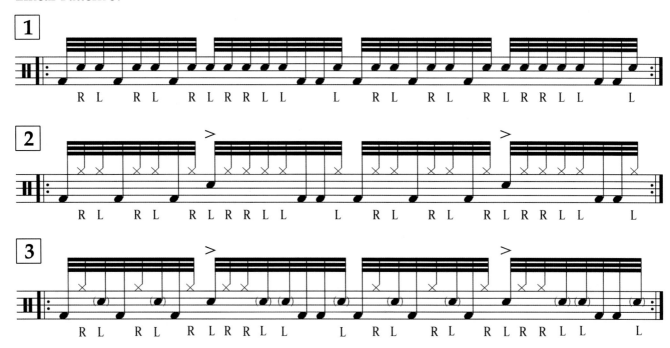

Linear Pattern 4:

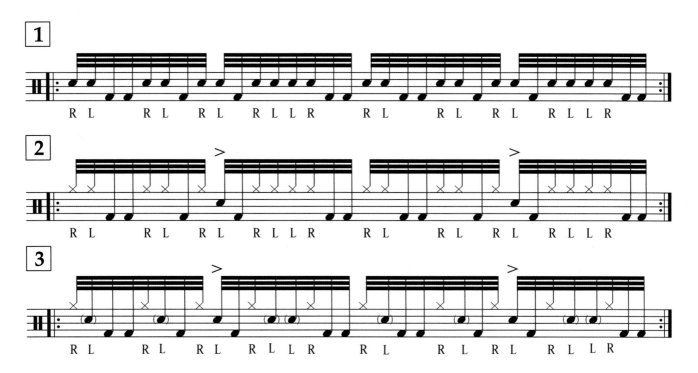

Grooves & Styles 2

AUDIO TRACK
#5

Drum and Bass (D'n'B for short), jungle and breakbeats are styles of electronic music that originated in England in the early 1990s. They are based on fast funk and breakbeats with tempos of approx. 150 to 190 bpm. Drum and Bass is still very popular in the DJ and club scene today.

The two most popular Drum and Bass Grooves are:

Artists (selecction):
Goldie, Pendulum, Squarepusher, Aphex Twin, The Chemical Brothers, DJ Rap, LTJ Bukem, Metrik, Sub Focus, Camo & Krooked, Wilkinson

Tip: There are also drum and bass artists who play live with drummers like Nerve with Jojo Mayer or Goldie & The Heritage Orchestra. Definitely recommendable!

Amen Break

The Amen Break is a good introduction to the world of breakbeats. It is one of the most sampled beats and is from the song "Amen, Brother" by the soul band "The Winstons" from 1969.

21

Breakbeats

AUDIO TRACK #6

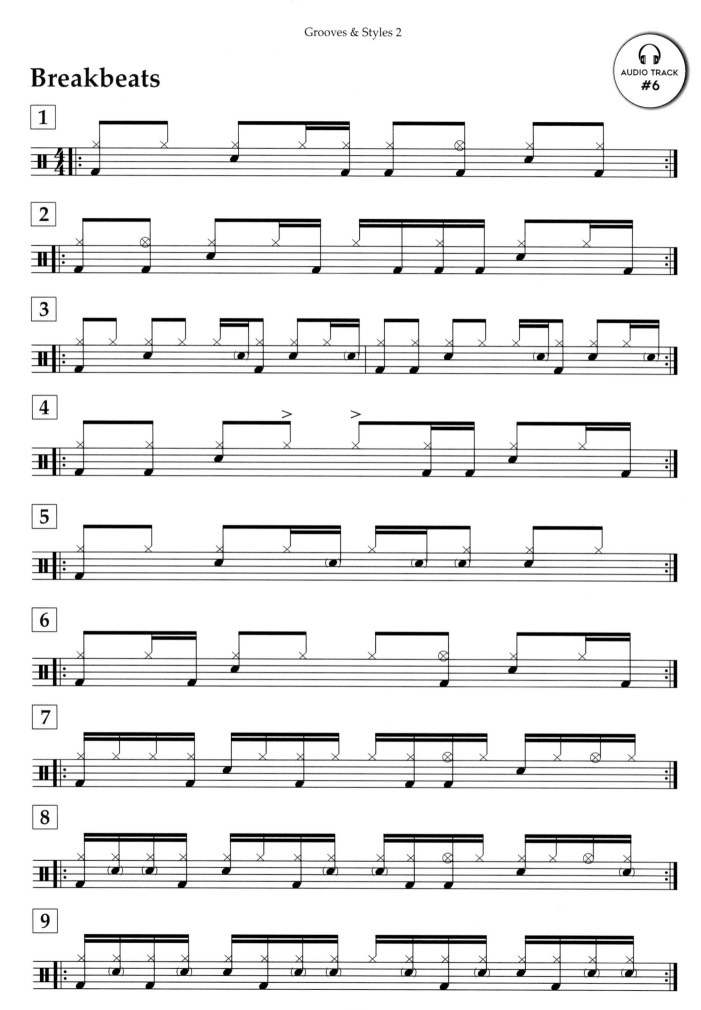

Jungle Grooves

Ostinatos 1

AUDIO TRACK #8

Figures of 3s 16ths with the feet:

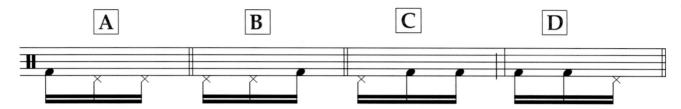

Hand patterns:

Start the figure of 3s with the simple eighth Groove as in the examples A - D below.

Then combine them with the following hand patterns 1 - 4 :

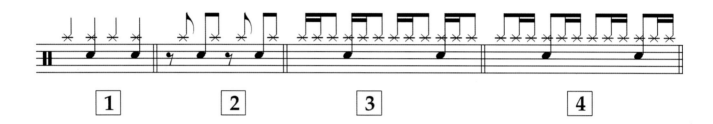

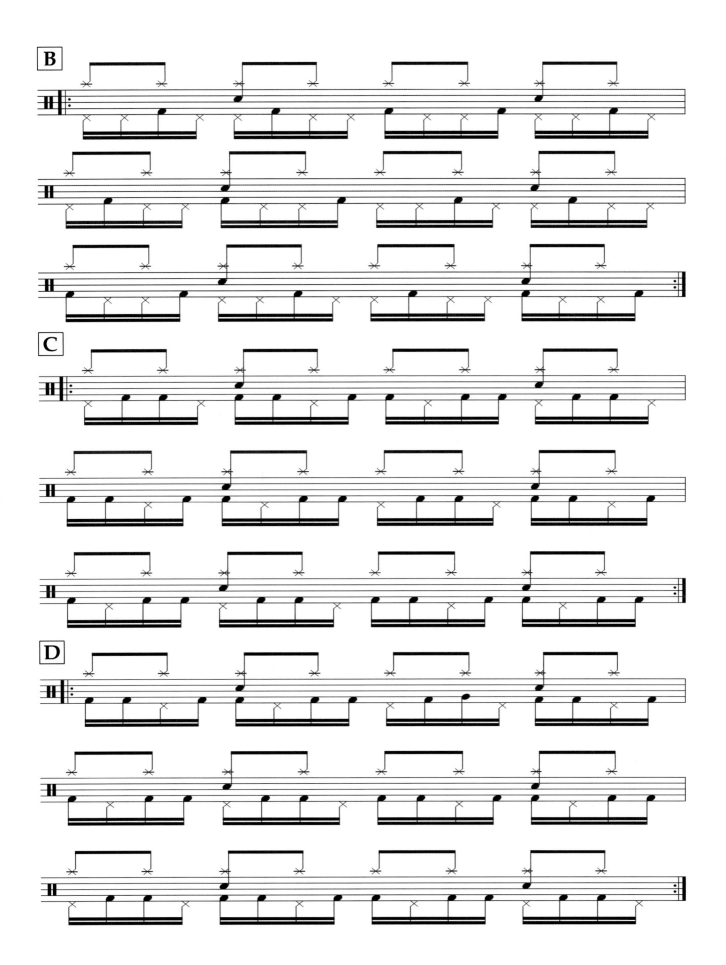

Improvisation 1

AUDIO TRACK
#9

Improvisation means performing something impromptu and without preparation. The word comes from the Italian word "improvviso", which means unforeseen, unexpected. In a musical context, it means that sequences of sounds emerge during the performance itself.

Exercise 1
Improvise in the first bar and repeat the improvisation in the second bar.

- Start with a very simple melody and play increasingly complex figures.
- Let the left foot run along on the quarter
- Make sure to repeat the first bar exactly

improvisation   **repetition**

Exercise 2
Improvise two bars and repeat both bars.

- Start as simple as possible and remember exactly what you have played
- Keep your left foot on the quarter
- Make sure you always keep good form

improvisation bar 1   **improvisation bar 2**

repetition
2

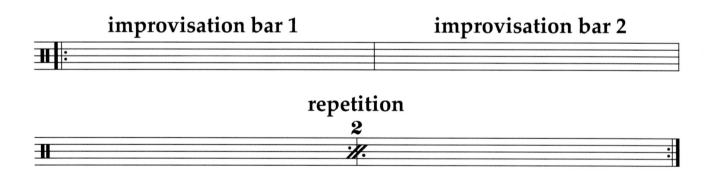

Tip: The exercises are also a lot of fun, especially in pairs, e.g. in a teacher-student situation. Each person can improvise freely or try to copy the other person's improvisation.

Polyrhythmics 1

The term refers to the simultaneous flow of two or more time signatures in the same measure of time. Especially in rock, jazz and fusion music, polyrhythm is often used.

Poly (Greek) = many, several
Ryhthmus (Greek) = equal measure; time division inserted into the bar metre, which is exactly determined by note values.

A good way to illustrate polyrhytmics is to show the beats within a table: first multiply the number of beats of the bars you want to connect to get the number of columns in the table. Then the beats are entered at intervals of their respective values.

Example 5 over 3:

5 * 3 = 15

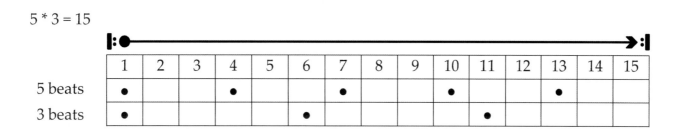

Example 3 over 2:

3 * 2 = 6

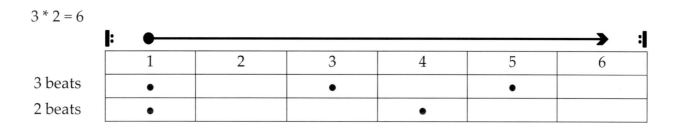

Go through the exercises on the next pages carefully and use a metronome. Start at a slow tempo, e.g. with the quarter notes at 70 bpm.

6 over 4

The polyrhythm 6 over 4 can be understood as a 6/4 bar that corresponds in duration to a 4/4 bar played simultaneously. It can also be understood as quarter triplets over a 4/4 bar.

6 over 4 is often used in music and you should always be able to count the six and the four.

$6 * 4 = 24$

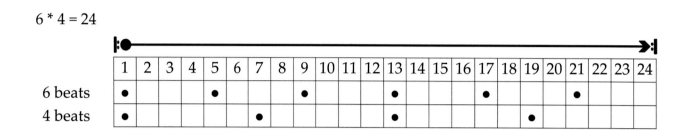

	1	2	3	4	5	6	7	8	9	10	11	12	13	14	15	16	17	18	19	20	21	22	23	24
6 beats	●				●				●				●				●				●			
4 beats	●						●						●						●					

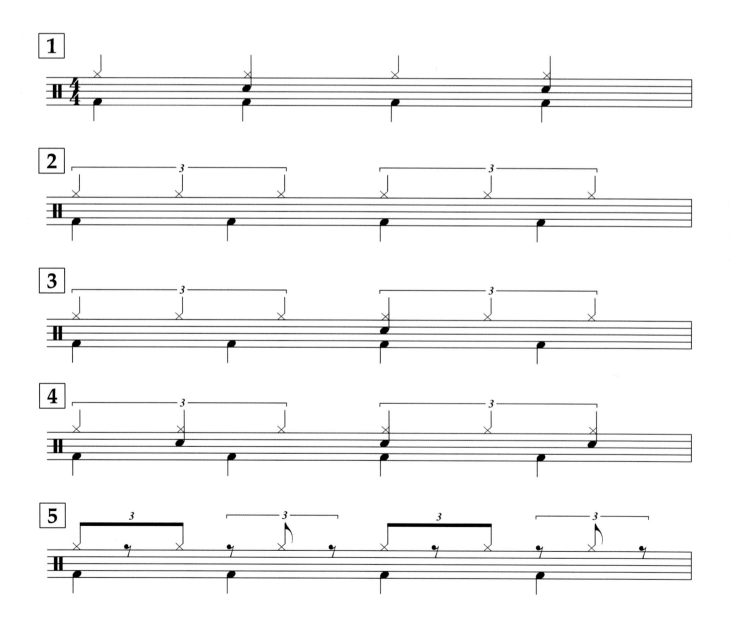

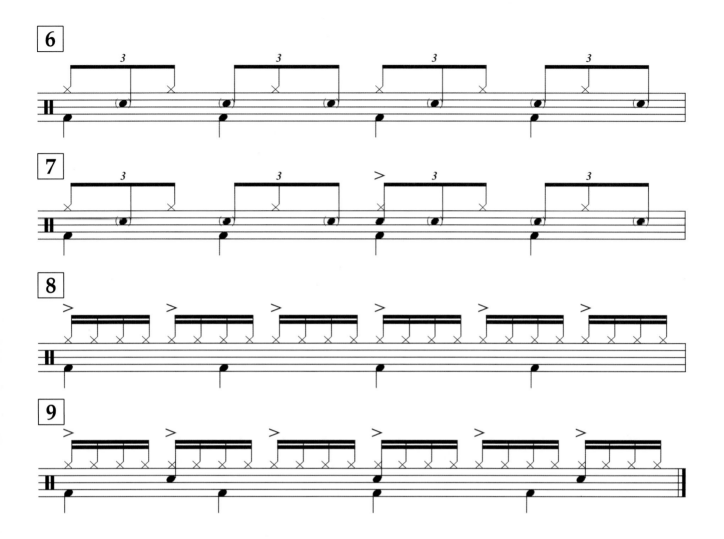

3 over 4

With this polyrhythm there are again several possibilities to define it:

• As a 3/4 bar, which corresponds in duration to a simultaneously played 4/4 bar
• Half triplets over a 4/4 bar

Practise to count the triple and quadruple divisions.

3 * 4 = 12

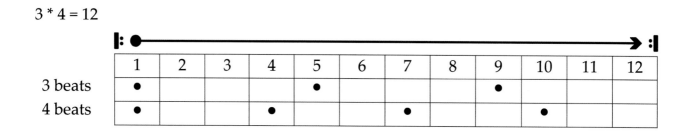

	1	2	3	4	5	6	7	8	9	10	11	12
3 beats	●				●				●			
4 beats	●			●			●			●		

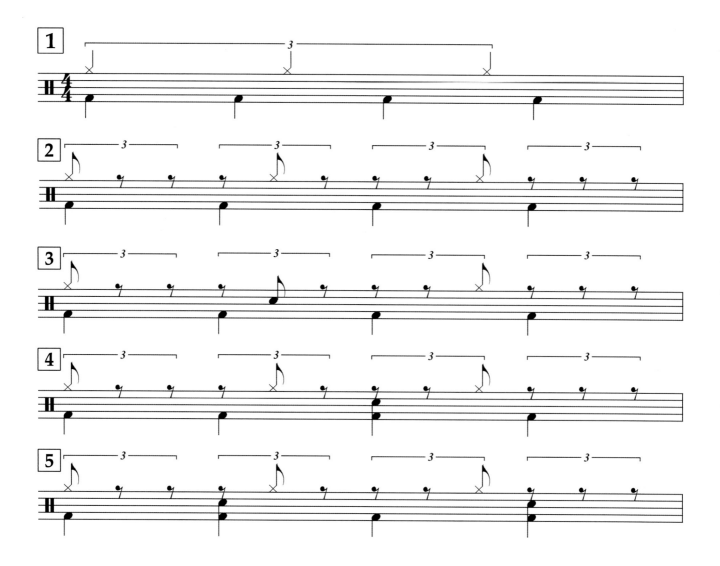

With Eighth Notes (6 over 8):

With Sixteenth Notes:

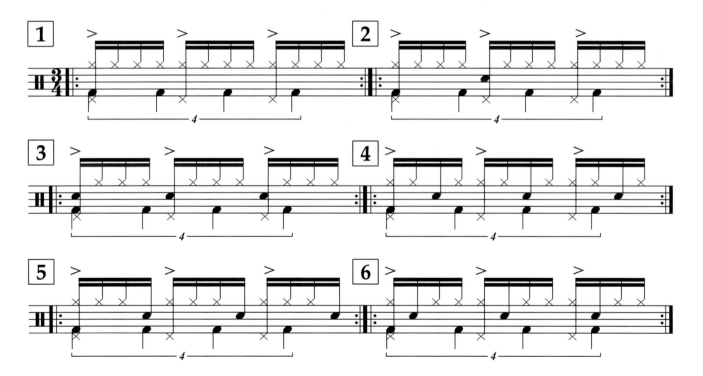

More Polyrhythms:

2 over 3

- Half notes of a 4/4 bar over a 3/4 bar
- Duols in a 3/4 bar
- Eighth notes over eighth triplets

$2 * 3 = 6$

	1	2	3	4	5	6
2 beats	●			●		
3 beats	●		●		●	

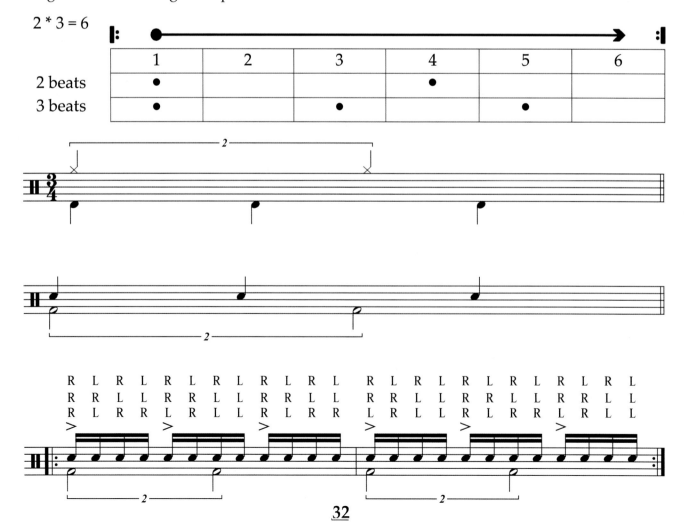

5 over 4

- A 5/4 bar is played simultaneously with a 4/4 bar
- Quintuplets over a grid of normal sixteenth notes

5 * 4 = 20

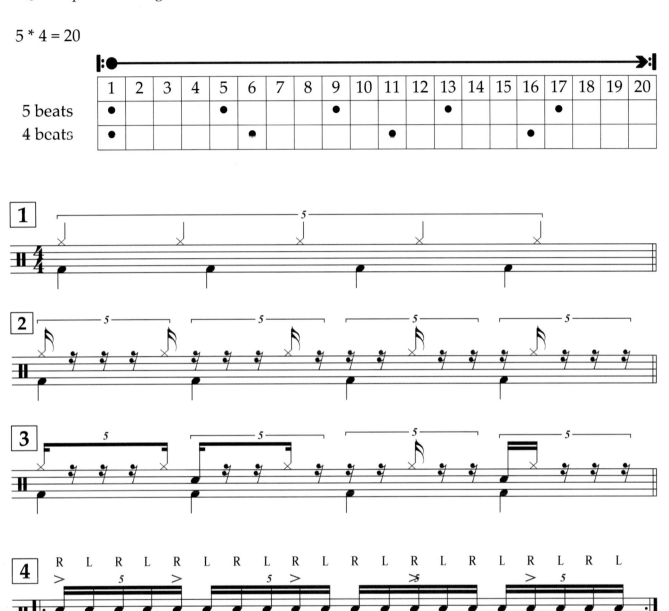

	1	2	3	4	5	6	7	8	9	10	11	12	13	14	15	16	17	18	19	20
5 beats	●				●				●				●				●			
4 beats	●					●					●					●				

Snare Drum Solo 2

32nd on the Set 2

The focus is on 32nd notes on the Hi-Hat.

• Try different stickings, the 32nds can often be played as singles or doubles

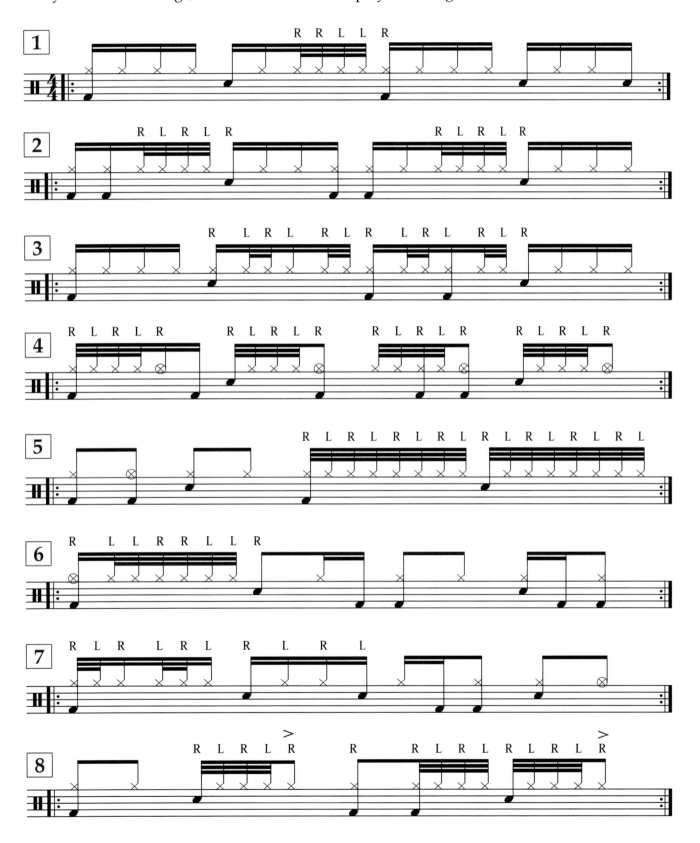

35

Licks 3

WATCH ONLINE

AUDIO TRACK #13

The 9 Lick

Grouping of 9 in 16th, sixtuplets and 32nd notes.

Sticking: R l l K K R L K K

In 16ths grid:

In a sixtuplet grid with stepped eighth notes on the Hi-Hat:

In four-bar patterns with Grooves:

- Play the Hi-Hat with the left foot in quarters, eighths and in the eighths offbeat
- The last quarter is filled with 32nd notes

In a 32nd note grid with stepped eighth notes on the Hi-Hat:

In four-bar patterns with Grooves:

Grooves & Styles 3

Samba

Samba refers to a style of music from Brazil and is the generic term for different types of music such as the samba enredo at carnival or the rural samba de roda. Samba is a very joyful music that fuses the dance and music of Afro-Brazilian culture.

Preliminary Exercises:

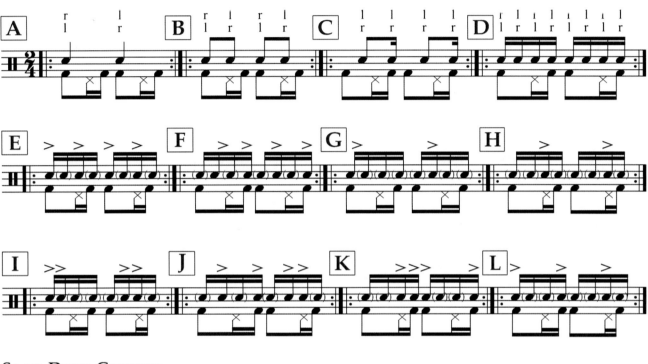

Snare Drum Grooves:

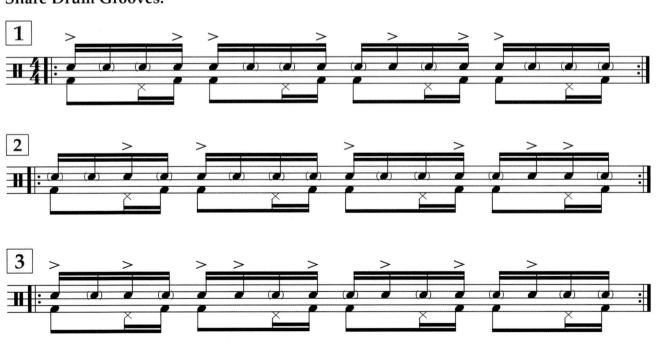

39

With Tom Toms:

With Ride Figure and Sidestick:

More Grooves:

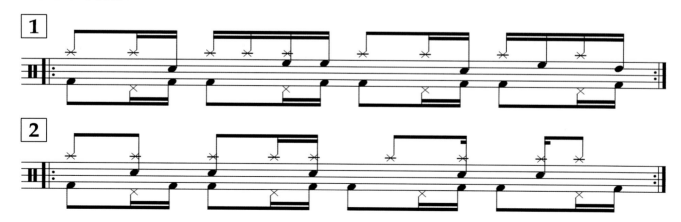

Latin

Latin music (German: lateinamerikanische Musik; Spanish: música latina) is the generic term for numerous musical styles originating from the Spanish- and Portuguese-speaking countries of the Americas. Typical representatives are rumba, mambo, bossanova, Afro-Cuban, reggae, samba, salsa, merengue, tango, calypso and bachata.

Unlike the European musical tradition, which tends to be based on a steady quarter pulse, the pulse of Latin music is called a clave (German: Schlüssel). The two most common claves are the son and rumba clave.

• Play half notes and quarter notes with the left foot
• Clap the clave

Son Clave

Rumba Clave

Famous Latin Drummers:

Horacio „El Negro" Hernandez, Alex Acuña, Walfredo Reyes Jr., Tito Puente, Antonio Sanchez, Dafnis Prieto, Bobby Sanabria, Jimmy Branly

Famous artists:

Harry Belafonte, Michel Camilo, Eddie Palmieri, Santana, Johnny Pacheco, Celia Cruz, Salsa Kings, Lou Bega, Mono Blanco, Gloria Estefan, Bob Marley, Peter Tosh, Desmond Dekker, Jimmy Cliff, Buena Vista Social Club, Ibrahim Ferrer etc.

Cuban Basics

Son Clave:

With Cascara:

With Bongo Bell:

Mambo Muntuno Bell:

Rumba Clave:

With Cascara:

With Bongo Bell:

Mambo Muntuno Bell:

Ostinati with the feet:

straight   bombo note   tumbao   baion

Cascara with Tumbao

Cascara:

With Tumbao:

With Hi-Hat:

With Bombo Note:

With Tumbao feet:

With Baion feet:

Tip: To train the coordination of the bass drum with the Cascara and Tumbao hand pattern properly, it is recommended to go through all the eighth note positions with one and two connected notes individually. The right and left hands and the hi-hat always remain the same and the bass drum plays the 1, then the 1+, the 2, the 2+ and so on. With two notes, then the 1 and the 1+, the 1+ and the 2, the 2 and the 2+, etc.

This is called a Permutation Exercise and will hep you with coordination and independence.

Afro-Cuban 6/8

The 4/4 clave most probably developed from the 6/8 clave. The 6/8 clave can be heard in many traditional African rhythms, some of which are centuries old.

Bembe Bell:

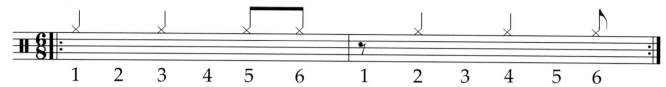

Bembe Bell: with 6/8 Clave

- Play the Bembe Bell with one of the eight Snare Drum accompaniments.
- Play all eight Snare Drum accompaniments with the four Bass Drum/Hi-Hat patterns

Snare Drum accompaniment:

Bassdrum/Hi-Hat Patterns:

Cha Cha

Cha Cha is a cheerful ballroom dance from Cuba danced in pairs.

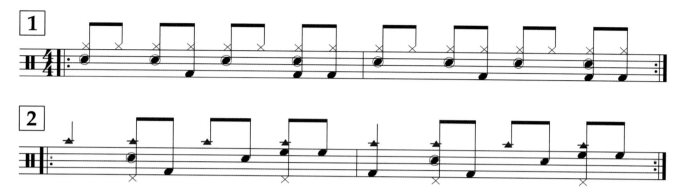

Mambo

Mambo is a type of music that developed in Cuba from 1930 onwards, as well as the name for the associated dance that developed parallel to the music. A very well-known piece is Mambo No. 5, which was covered by Lou Bega, among others.

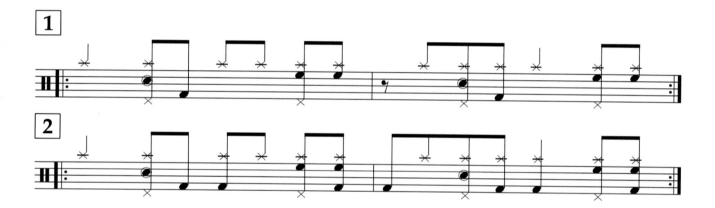

Mozambique

This style also comes from the country of the same name in Africa. Music and dance are an integral part of everyday life in Mozambique. They are an expression of happiness and unhappiness and are also used as a weapon of war in conflicts.

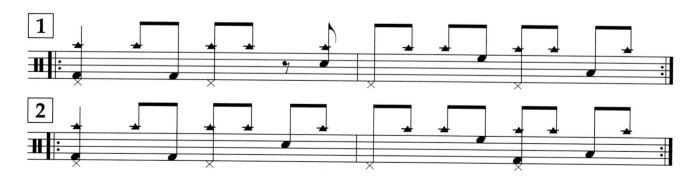

Songo

Changuito, percussionist of the Cuban group Los Van Van, developed the songo in the 1960s.

Naningo

Naningo comes from the Brazilian Candomblé tradition and is a mystical offshoot of samba.

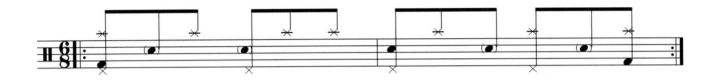

Merengue

Merengue [me'reŋge] (Spanish for "meringue", "meringue") is a music style from the Dominican Republic and also refers to the associated dance.

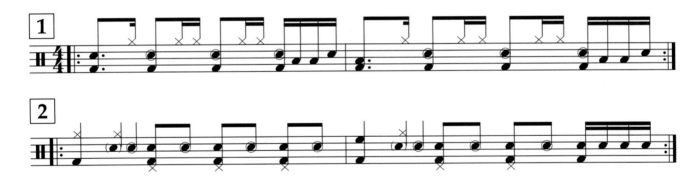

Bolero

Bolero is a Latin American music, dance and song form in straight time. A famous work with this name is also the Bolero by Maurice Ravel.

Soca

Soca is a music genre that originated in Trinidad and Tobago in the early 1970s from calypso and influences from soul, funk and Indian instruments.

Tango

Tango is a music genre and dance from Argentina.

Calypso

Calypso is an Afro-Caribbean dance rhythm and music style. One of the most famous representatives is, for example, Harry Belafonte.

Reggae

Reggae is one of the most important styles of popular music that emerged in Jamaica at the end of the 1960s. A famous representative for example is Bob Marley.

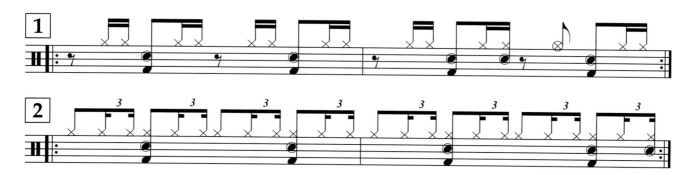

Improvisation 2

WATCH ONLINE

AUDIO TRACK #18

Replace and Orchestrate

The following improvisation exercise is about consciously staying in a subdivision. Replace strokes with the hands by the feet and distribute them over the drum kit. Try every possible combination you know.

- Try to play all possible hand/foot combinations of a subdivision
- Stay longer in one subdivision and consciously switch to the next one
- Do not mix subdivisions
- Play the subdivisions down and up again
- Let the Hi-Hat run along on the quarter note

Tip: Always record yourself and listen back to it! That is one of the best ways to get valuable feedback. There is no expensive equipment needed, a mobile phone can do the job.

Coordination 2

- Play the Bass Drum to the patterns A-D with the notes from the "Reading text melody"
- Groove with the patterns beforehand
- Sing or speak the notes during the pattern
- Play each bar individually in the loop, then whole lines and at the end the section completely

Inward Doubles Patterns:

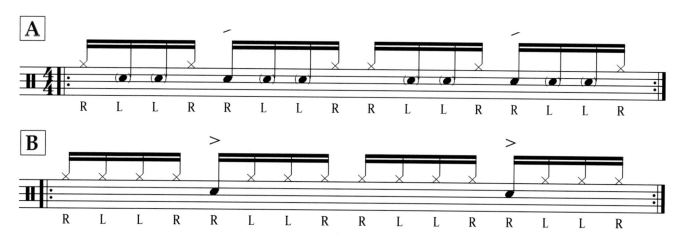

Inward Paradiddle/Paradiddle Pattern:

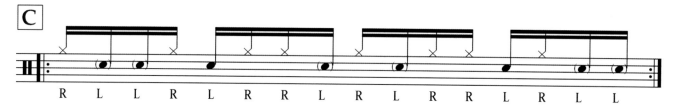

Ghost Note Pattern:

Paradiddle Diddle Diddle Pattern:

Reading Text Melody

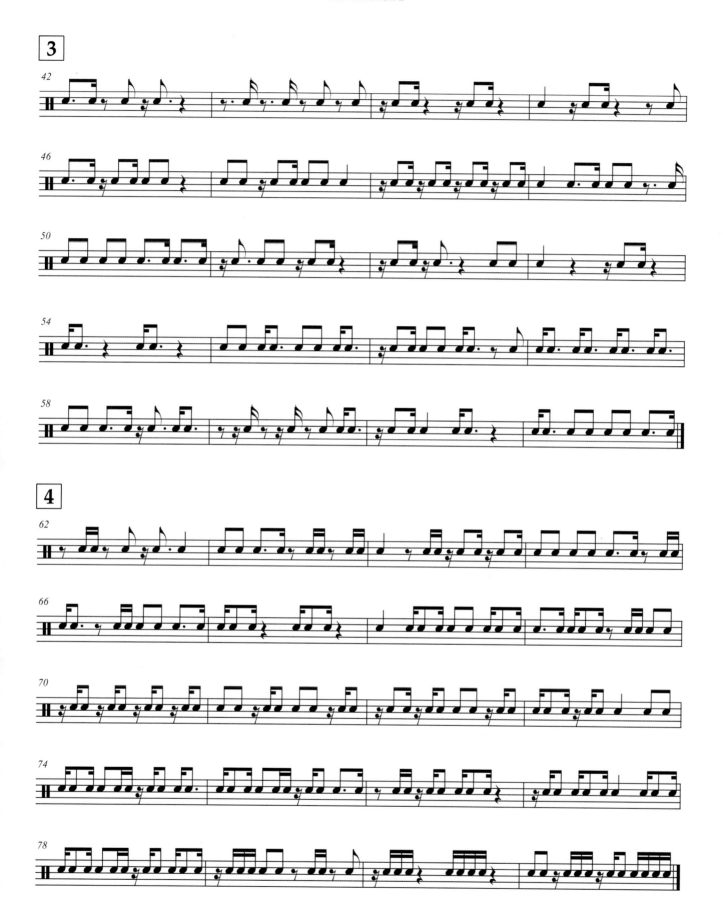

Licks 4

AUDIO TRACK #19

- Practice the figures slowly at first and with metronome
- Then play the licks alternating with grooves

32nd Linear Lick

Beat 1 in 16ths:

Beat 2 and 3 in 16ths:

Beat 4 in 16ths:

32nd Groove Lick

With a stop on beat 3:

32nd Groove Lick 2

R L R L R L   R L   R L

Step 1:

R L R L R L

Step 2:

R L R L R L   R L

Toms Backwards Lick

R L R L R L R L R L R R L L R L R R L L R L R R L L R L R

Step 1:

R L R L R L R L

Step 2:

R L R L R L R L R R L L R L R R

Step 3:

R L R L R L R L R L R R L L R L R R L L R L R R L L R L R L L

Paradiddle Diddle (Diddle) Lick

AUDIO TRACK #20

- The lick consists of two patterns with 8 and 12 notes each
- At the beginning the pattern with 12 notes is slightly varied to: K LLRRLLRR
- Start slowly and practise with metronome
- Play the Lick alternating with grooves

The complete Lick as 32nd notes over two bars:

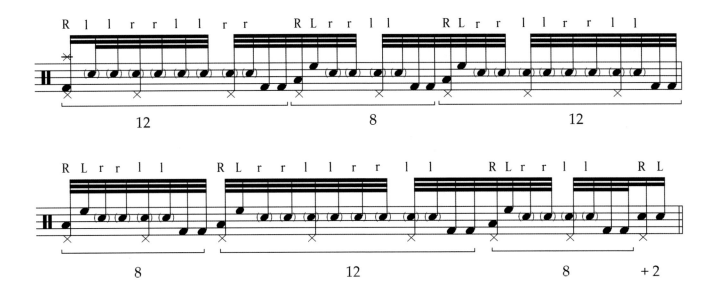

Illustrated in 16th grid:

1. Variation at the beginning:

Sticking: K LLRRLLRR KK

2. Eight note grouping in 16th note grid:

Sticking: R L R R L L KK

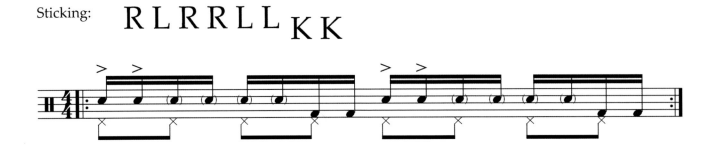

3. Twelve note grouping in 16th note grid:

Sticking: **R L R R L L R R L L** K K

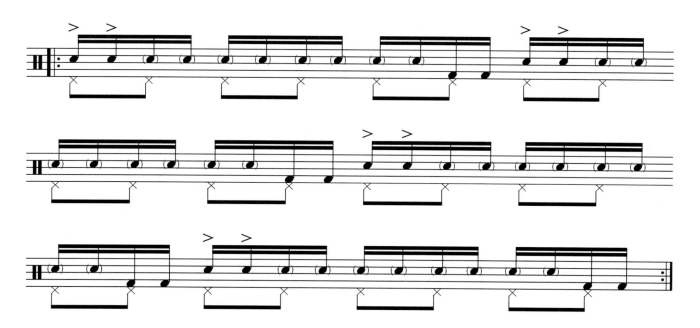

3. With variation and tom-toms on the singles:

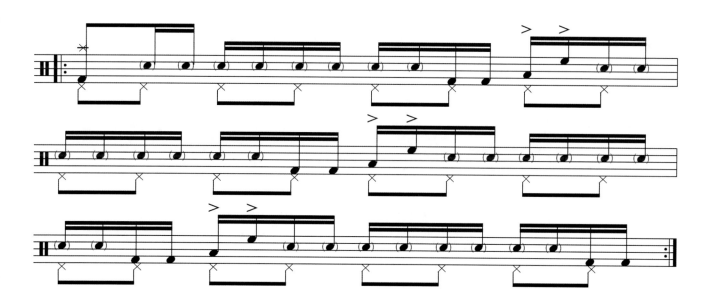

Hand/Foot Single Rolls

Single Pyramid:

- Play the pyramid with the right hand only and with the left hand only as well as right and left - alternately and simultaneously
- Play the pyramid on the floor tom as well
- Practice with metronome
- Start with the foot as an alternative exercise only in the second bar after a note value change

Single Rolls Fill Ins:

• Practice the Fill Ins alternating with Grooves
• Bring the Fill Ins also to high tempi
• Let the Hi-Hat run along on the quarters

Hand/Foot Double Rolls

- Play the pyramid only with right, left and right and left hand alternately
- Play the pyramid also on the floor tom
- Practice with a metronome

Doubles Pyramid:

Inward Doubles Pyramid:

Ostinatos 2

- The ostinato A, B or C runs through constantly with the feet
- Alternate with all hand movements and try to play the notes in all hand movements
  (RLRL, LRLR, RRLL, LLRR, RLRR LRLL etc.)
- Groove a few bars with the ostinato before you start with the notes
- Sing or speak the notes in advance to the ostinato

Polyrhythmics 2

3s Shift Hi-Hat

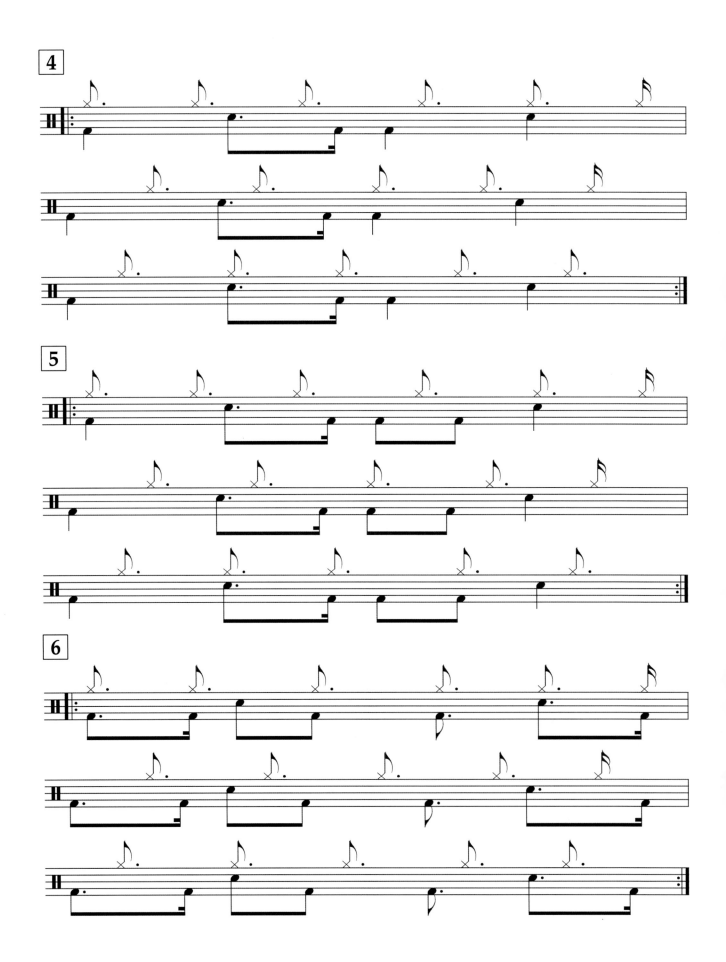

5s Shift Hi-Hat

AUDIO TRACK #24

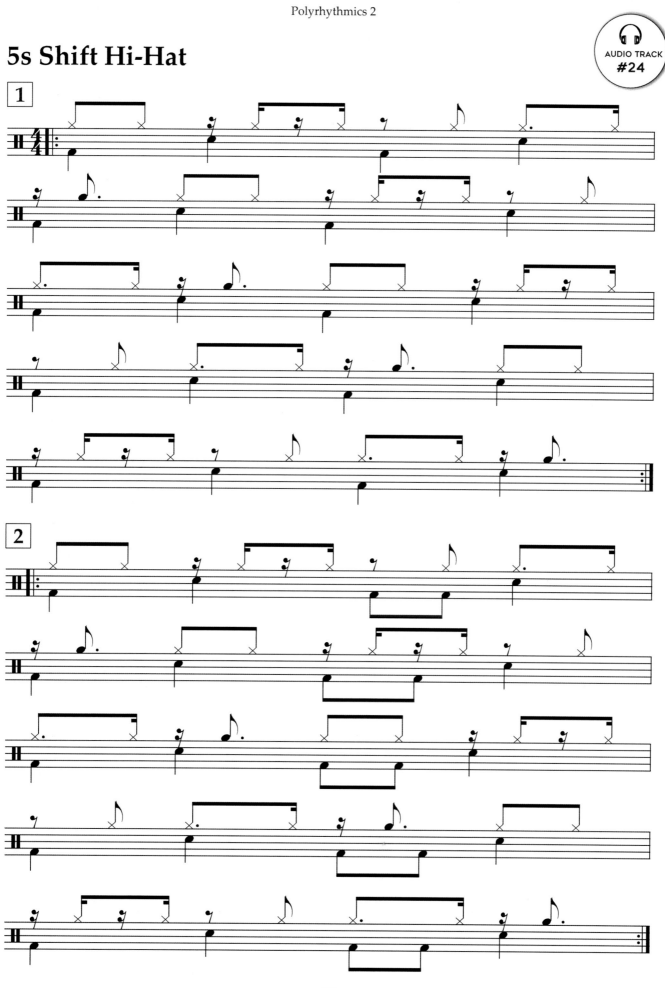

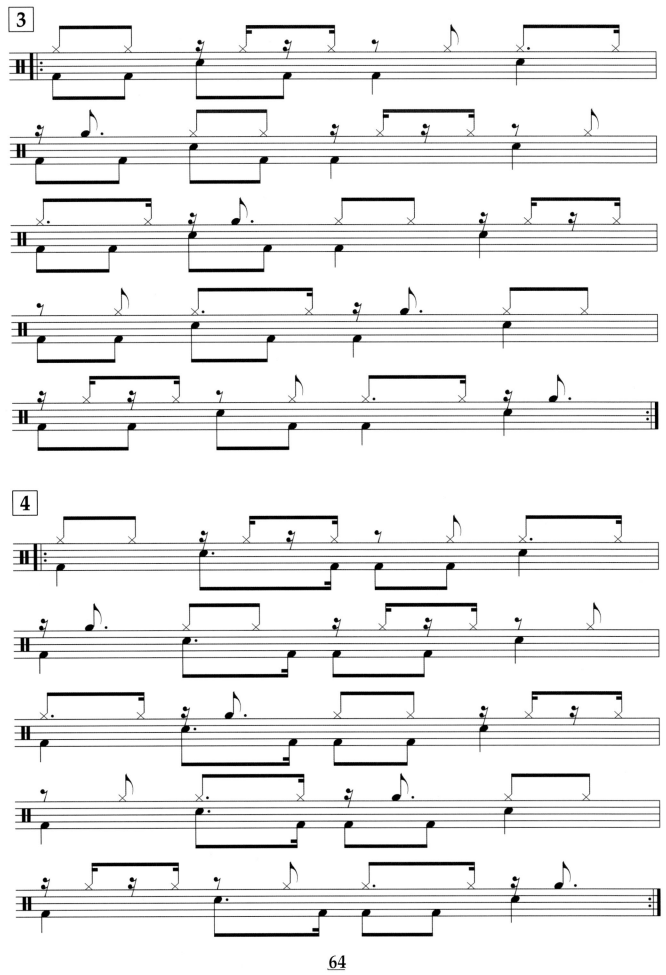

Drumsolo

Playing drum solos is considered the supreme discipline on the drums. The basic purpose of a solo is to show what you can play on the drums. In addition, entertaining the audience, a skilful progression of tension and a comprehensible structure contribute to a successful solo. A great solo inspires the audience and helps to build a good reputation as an artist. On top of that, it's just really fun to express yourself creatively. To play a good performance, you need experience, technique, creativity and a plan. You should know what you want and not just play at it. Free playing can work, but it needs a lot of improvisational talent and experience. It is better to have a plan with a precise goal.

You can compare this well with an aeroplane taking off. There is always a goal that has been set beforehand. You never just fly off and buzz around until you run out of fuel at the end. You set yourself a thematic thread with a beginning and a goal and think carefully about what happens in between. Where do I want to go? How do I get there? What do I want to express? These questions should be answered before you start.

Other characteristics can be identified in a successful solo:

Timing
The solo has a continuous pulse emanating from the hi-hat, bass drum or both.

Dynamics
With different volumes you can create much more tension with constant rhythms than if everything "runs through" at one volume. The quieter you play, the more carefully you have to listen.

Repetitions
If you just randomly play one lick after another, the repetition is missing for the listener. Repetition is important to create recognition and make the lick more tangible and understandable.

I distinguish between different types of solos, which I will go into in more detail in the next pages. These cannot stand 100% on their own, as many of them share commonalities and elements merge into each other.

Of course, for drum solos, "practice makes perfect" also applies. Keep at it, and don't give up if it doesn't sound the way you want it to at the beginning. Especially then it should motivate you to keep working on it until the solo meets your expectations.

Tip: Be sure to record your solos! This is the only way to get honest feedback and to work effectively on the parts that do not yet correspond to your sound ideas. You don't need a lot of technology for this, a smartphone is often enough. To counteract overmodulation at high volume, the input level should be lowered or, for example, a towel should be placed in front of or on top of the microphone.

Soloing over Kicks (Vamps)

The term comes from jazz and refers to a recurring accompaniment figure over which improvisation takes place. In musical terms, it is an ostinato. The term is also used in blues, soul and R&B and there are numerous songs based on it. One of the most famous is, for example, "Hit the Road Jack" by Ray Charles.

• Try to catch the kicks in general
• Play all kinds of Grooves and Licks over them and also change the subdivision
• Give it your all and really go for it
• Record your solos, the audio tracks can also be dragged into a DAW for this purpose
• Each vamp is available in 80, 90 and 100 bpm as an audio track

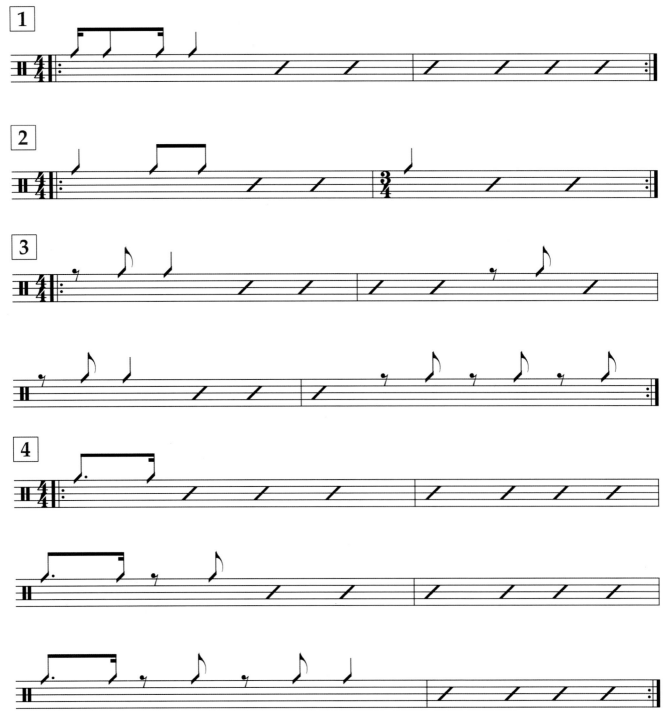

Homebase Solo

As a home base, you choose a groove, a melody or a pattern to which you return again and again during the solo. When returning, the home base can be played the same or slightly changed with a variation. The excursions and events in between are freely arranged or planned.

The home base can always remain the same as in example 1 or vary as in example 2.

Example 1:

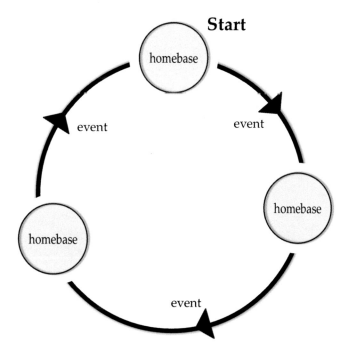

Example 2:

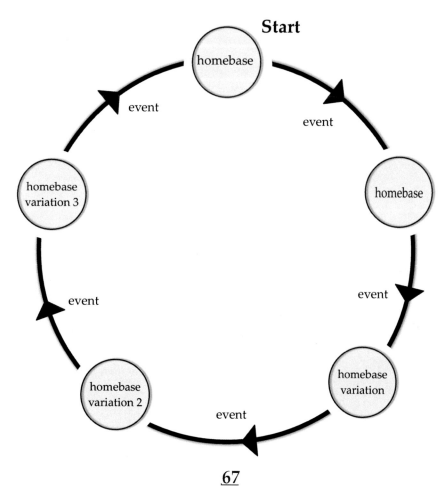

Song form Solo

With this type of solo, you proceed as with a piece of music. There are different parts, grooves and climaxes that run in sequence. The sequence should be written down in advance and the lengths of the parts should be determined by the number of bars.

Example:

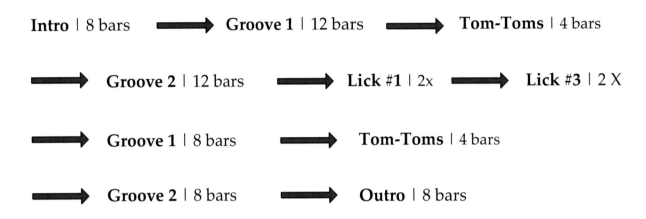

Intro | 8 bars ⟶ **Groove 1** | 12 bars ⟶ **Tom-Toms** | 4 bars

⟶ **Groove 2** | 12 bars ⟶ **Lick #1** | 2x ⟶ **Lick #3** | 2 X

⟶ **Groove 1** | 8 bars ⟶ **Tom-Toms** | 4 bars

⟶ **Groove 2** | 8 bars ⟶ **Outro** | 8 bars

Instrument based Solo

In approaching the solo, one proceeds according to the instruments and assigns them to certain sequences and parts.

Example:

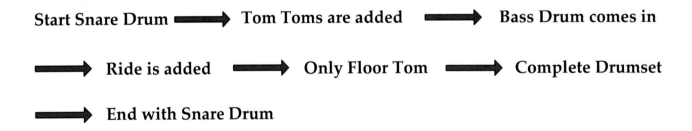

Start Snare Drum ⟶ **Tom Toms are added** ⟶ **Bass Drum comes in**

⟶ **Ride is added** ⟶ **Only Floor Tom** ⟶ **Complete Drumset**

⟶ **End with Snare Drum**

Tip: Both approaches can also be mixed well. Form and instruments can also be written down together.

Free Solo

With the free solo, you deliberately don't set yourself a framework and are actually "free". You play extemporaneously and let yourself be surprised where it takes you. There are no limits to creativity. Nevertheless, it is important to have a good sense of when which part creates a successful arc of tension in order to keep the solo interesting. You should also develop a good feeling for when the right time has come to find the exit and thus end the solo. When you have said everything, there is no point in continuing to speak, otherwise it will seem tiring to the listener.

Composed Solo

The composed solo can be seen as the opposite of the free solo. Here, the sequence and every beat is precisely defined. Preparation and notation beforehand require a lot of time, but it is the safest method for delivering a solo confidently in live situations. Especially in front of an audience, the notated solo can prevent you from getting stuck or blacking out. In addition, you have time to rehearse the solo in advance. After many repetitions, you usually know it by heart and have it so well anchored in your memory that you only have to recall it at the push of a button.

Note-taking is done in the classical way with sheet music and pencil. For those who like to work on the computer, notation software is of course recommended. The programmes Aared or Musescore are suitable for beginners. If you want to work more professionally on notation, Finale or Sybelius are recommended. To learn the more complex programmes, it is also worth booking a workshop.

„I Never play a drum solo you cant´t dance to."
Gene Krupa

„To me, drum soloing is like doing a marathon and solving equations at the same time."
Neil Peart

DRUMMER QUOTES

"I remember in the early days when we played six nights a week for a month and I was doing my long drum solo every night. My hands were covered in blisters."
John Bonham

„If you get stuck in a drum solo, just play rolls!"
Ian Paice

Groove Solo

In this type of solo, you play a specific Groove that you establish, vary and play around over the solo. With excursions to other Grooves, Licks and Fills, you return to the original Groove or a variation of it.

Solo Groove Examples:

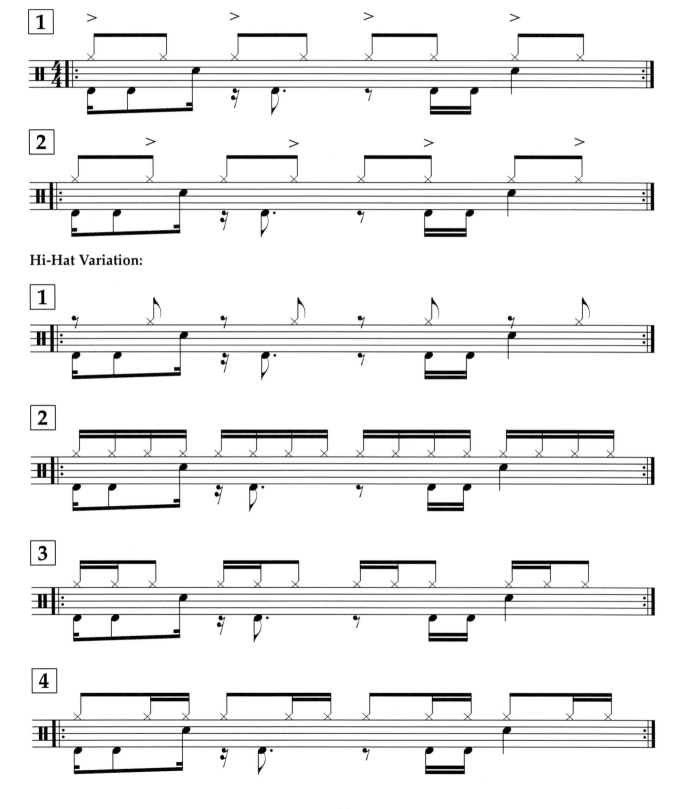

Hi-Hat Variation:

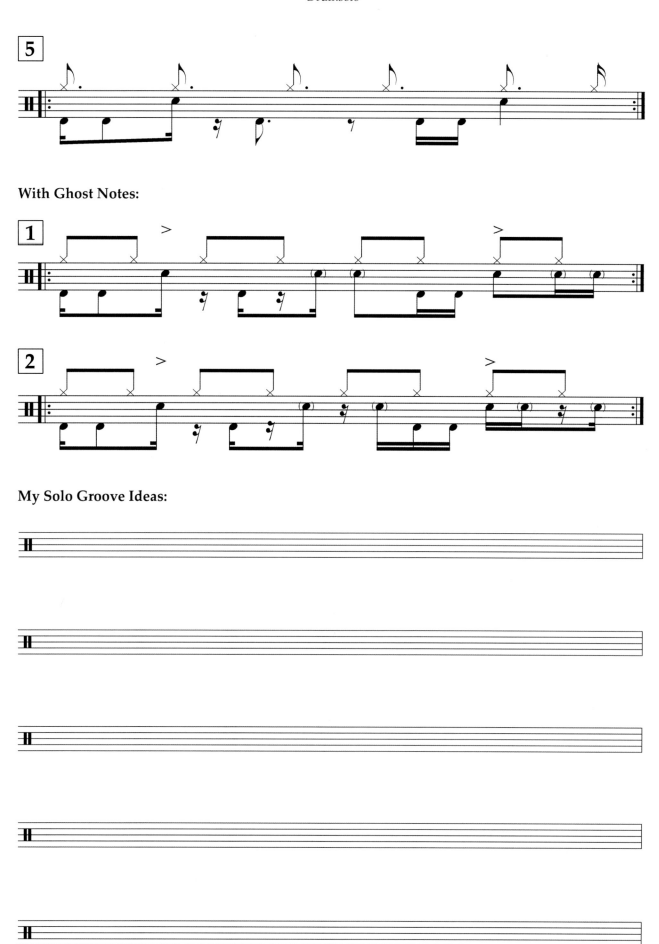

With Ghost Notes:

My Solo Groove Ideas:

The 40 PAS Rudiments
Noted by Kai-Ole Buuck

I. Roll Rudiments

A. Single Stroke Roll Rudiments

1. Single Stroke Roll

2. Single Stroke Four

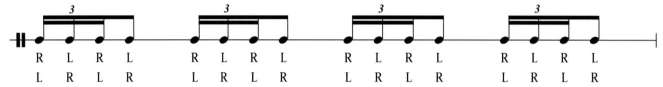

3. Single Stroke Seven

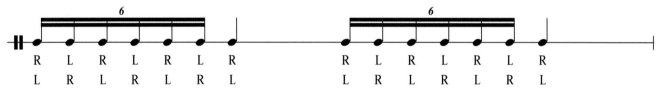

B. Multiple Bounce Roll Rudiments

4. Multiple Bounce Roll

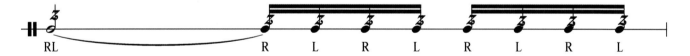

5. Triple Stroke Roll

C. Double Stroke Rudiments

6. Double Stroke Roll

1

7. Five Stroke Roll

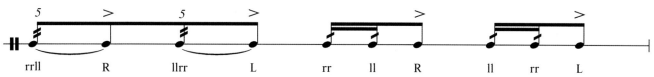

rrll   R   llrr   L   rr   ll   R   ll   rr   L

8. Six Stroke Roll

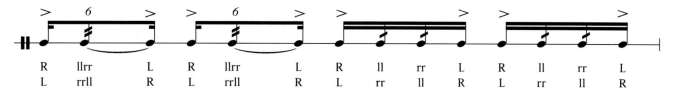

R   llrr   L   R   llrr   L   R   ll   rr   L   R   ll   rr   L
L   rrll   R   L   rrll   R   L   rr   ll   R   L   rr   ll   R

9. Seven Stroke Roll

rrllrr   L   rrllrr   L   rr   ll   rr   L   rr   ll   rr   L
llrrll   R   llrrll   R   ll   rr   ll   R   ll   rr   ll   R

10. Nine Stroke Roll

rrllrrll   R   llrrllrr   L   rr   ll   rr   ll   R   ll   rr   ll   rr   L

11. Ten Stroke Roll

rrllrrll   R L   llrrllrr   L R   rr   ll   rr   ll   R L   ll   rr   ll   rr   L R

12. Eleven Stroke Roll

rrllrrll   rr L   llrrllrr   ll R   rr   ll   rr   ll   rr   L   ll   rr   ll   rr   ll   R

13. Thirteen Stroke Roll

rrllrrll   rrll   R   llrrllrr   llrr   L   rr   ll   rr   ll   rr   ll   R   ll   rr   ll   rr   ll   rr   L

14. Fifteen Stroke Roll

rrllrrll   rrllrr   L rrllrrll   rrllrr   L   rr   ll   rr   ll   rr   ll   rr   L   rr   ll   rr   ll   rr   ll   rr   L
llrrllrr   llrrll   R llrrllrr   llrrll   R   ll   rr   ll   rr   ll   rr   ll   R   ll   rr   ll   rr   ll   rr   ll   R

15. Seventeen Stroke Roll

rrll..   R   llrr..   L   rr ll rr ll rr ll rr ll R   ll rr ll rr ll rr ll rr L

II. Diddle Rudiments

16. Single Paradiddle

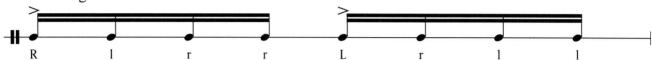

R   l   r   r   L   r   l   l

17. Double Paradiddle

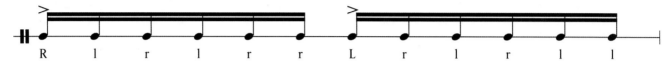

R l r l r r L r l r l l

18. Triple Paradiddle

R l r l r l r r L r l r l r l l

19. Paradiddlediddle

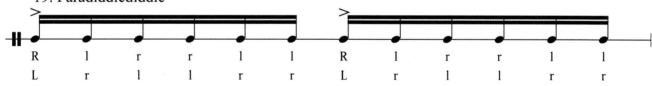

R l r r l l R l r r l l
L r l l r r L r l l r r

III. Flam Rudiments

Flam

l R   r L

Flam Accent

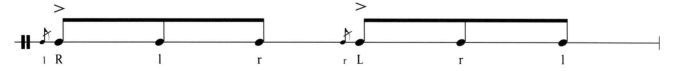

l R   l   r   r L   r   l

Flam Tap

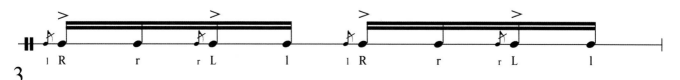

l R   r   r L   l   l R   r   r L   l

Flamacue
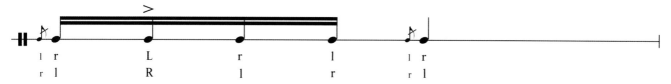

Flam Paradiddle
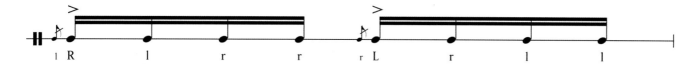

Single Flamed Mill
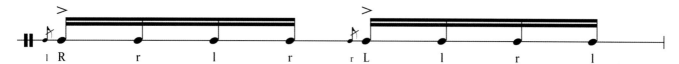

Flam Paradiddlediddle

Pataflafla
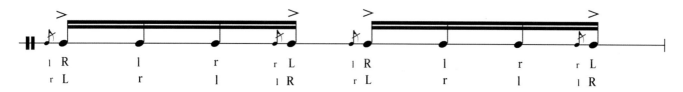

Swiss Army Triplet
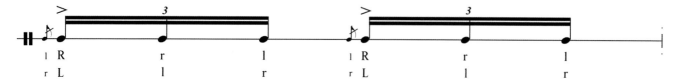

Inverted Flam Tap
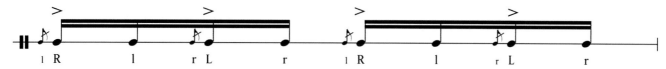

Flam Drag
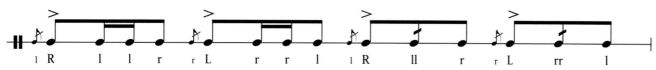

4

IV. Drag Rudiments

31. Drag

32. Single Drag Tap

33. Double Drag Tap

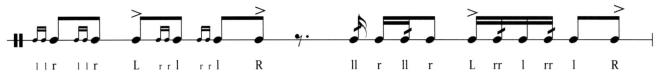

34. Lesson 25

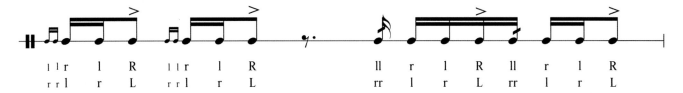

35. Single Dragadiddle

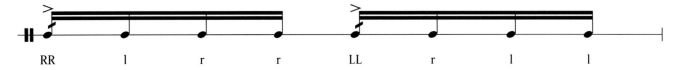

36. Drag Paradiddle #1

37. Drag Paradiddle #2

5

38. Ratamacue

l l r   l   r   L   r r l   r   l   R   ll   r   l   r   L   rr   l   r   l   R

39. Double Ratamacue

l l r   l l r   l   r   L   r r l   r r l   r   l   R   ll   r   ll   r   l   r   L   rr   l   rr   l   r   l   R

40. Triple Ratamacue

l l r   l l r   l l r   l   r   L r r l r r l r r l   r   l   R   ll   r   ll   r   ll   r   l   r   L   rr   l   rr   l   rr   l   r   l   R

Practice Log

Date	Topic/Exercise	Notes	Duration

Practice Log

Date	Topic/Exercise	Notes	Duration

Links:

www.rc-schneider.com

www.360drums.net

www.backbeat-studio.de

Many thanks to

Krista und Robert Schneider, Lisa Schneider, Hanno und Elisabeth Buchner, Thommy Buccini, Julia Stadler, Kai-Ole Buuck, Roland Depner, Christoph Zeller, Thomas Fleischmann, Boris Kounovsky, Matthias Hohmann, Perkussion Creativ e.V., Claus Hessler, Musication Nürnberg, Musik Klier, Andreas Moissl, Christoph Huber, Tommy Resch, Matthias Bäuerlein, AllEndsWell, Thomas Mayerl, Sven Struller, The Blackscreen, Fish and Scale, Money left to burn, Earth Flight, Caprize…

And of course you for reading and working with this book!

About the author

RC Schneider (**R**alph **C**hristian Schneider) studied at the Berufsfachschule für Musik in Nuremberg and Dinkelsbühl (state-certified ensemble leader in the field of rock/pop/jazz), is a graduate of the Professional Program Drums at the Future Music School and a specialist teacher for music and economics (graduated from the Staatsinstitut Ansbach).

He has played and worked with numerous artists and bands, including Not For Sale, Fish and Scale, The Blackscreen, Zen Meister, Midnight Sunrise, Stereotide, The Grand Astoria, Buzzride, Platinium, Money left to burn, Storm in The Attic, All Ends Well, Earth Flight and many more. Several concert tours have taken him to Austria, Switzerland, France, Poland, Czech Republic, Estonia, Latvia and Russia.

He has attended many workshops and masterclasses with Claus Hessler, Jojo Mayer, Dom Famularo, Jost Nickel, Anika Nilles, Gerwin Eisenhauer, Rick Latham, Walfrdo Reyes Jr, Moritz Müller, Oli Rubow, Roland Peil and Ricky Lawson, among others.

Since 2013 he has been giving drum and percussion courses at various secondary schools in the Nuremberg area and is also active there as a drum teacher in the „Klasse im Puls" project. In addition, he has been a drum teacher at one of the largest public schools for drums and percussion in the Nuremberg area, Roland Depner's Top Drum Studio, since 2015.

He was the founder and managing director of myinstrument - a social network specialised in musicians. Then in 2016 he founded Pro Cymbals, Germany's first service for professional drum cymbal reconditioning.

In 2017, he founded Backbeat Studio, where he offers drum lessons and works on music and video productions.

In 2020, he completed the audio engineering course "Hofa Pro" and successfully passed the exam to become a certified audio engineer.

In 2021 he founded 360 Drums, a modern publisher and online shop all about drums and percussion. There he publishes his books and products, and offers courses and workshops.

youtube.com/@rcsdrums   instagram.com/rcsdrums   facebook.com/rcsdrums

"Learning to play the drums is a wonderful journey that never ends. Enjoy the ride with all the ups and downs!"

All the best & good luck!

Online Videos

@RCSDRUMS

Licks 3

The 9 Lick, page 36 - 37

Improvisation 2

Replace and Orchestrate, page 48

Grooves & Styles 3

Samba, page 39 - 40

MORE PUBLICATIONS AVAILABLE FROM 360 DRUMS

Book 1 and 2 of the series **Learn Drums with Lesson Plan**:

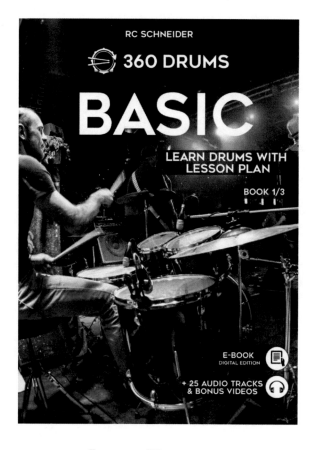

Learn Drums
BASIC
Book 1/3

Paperback
ISBN 978-3-949357-14-5

Learn Drums
ADVANCED
Book 2/3

Paperback
ISBN 978-3-949357-15-2

WWW.360DRUMS.NET

PRO

LEARN DRUMS WITH LESSON PLAN

1st edition 2023

Paperback edition

ISBN 978-3-949357-16-9

360 Drums

Willy-Spilling-Weg 17

90455 Nürnberg | Germany

www.360drums.net | mail@360drums.net

Made in the USA
Middletown, DE
02 August 2023

36121788R00049